The 9ᵗʰ Question

Dan Wyson, CFP®

Cover Design by Jaimee Lee

About the Author

Dan Wyson, CFP® received his formal education at BYU and then went on to receive his designation as a Certified Financial Planner™ professional.

Dan has written a weekly newspaper column that has been published through the Gannet/USA Today Network in Cities all over the country, totaling more than 800 original columns. He is also author of "21 Financial Myths", a guide to some of the errors that have crept into the thinking of today's investors. He has written two children's books, "The Gold Egg" and "The Magic Violin" which seek to inspire young people to pursue their dreams.

Dan's writing style displays his unique ability to put complex problems into simple and entertaining terms, so that all readers will find their understanding of the investing process greatly improved.

Dan and his talented wife Launa have 12 lovely children and are grandparents to an ever-increasing number of adorable grandchildren. Their family is the focus of their life and you will find several of them working at the family firm - Wyson Financial/Wealth Management.

"The 9th Question" is the result of decades of meeting with individuals and families about their investments and helping them solve their most pressing questions. The ultimate goal is to help people find more peace in their life by helping them follow sound financial and investing principles.

Introduction – *(Don't go skipping this part)*

When I was a child I talked a lot. At least that's how my mom remembered it. One day I was following her around asking about various matters that were on my mind. I'm not sure specifically what it was but knowing me it probably had to do with why clouds don't fall to the ground, how a swarm of birds kept from bumping into each other, or why words weren't always spelled the way they sounded. I asked that last one a lot. Whatever it was, on this particular day she got a little frustrated and said, in a slightly elevated voice, "Danny, you sure have a lot of questions today." After a moment of thought I replied, "I'm not even asking most of them."

I remember having a mind that questioned just about everything. Before I was a teen my parents bought one of those huge A-Z encyclopedias. I remember my mom telling me that now I could find answers to all my questions, and I did. One of my favorite activities in my youth was reading those books one "letter" at a time. I loved learning and wanted to know how everything in the world worked. As I got older my love for learning grew into a love of teaching. I suppose I might have pursued a career in education, but somewhere along the way someone must have told me that a teacher would never be able to afford an airplane so that was simply a non-starter in my aviation obsessed mind. But that story is for another book.

As a Certified Financial Planner™ professional, I have constant opportunities to both learn and teach. I have found that many times I learn the most while I am teaching, which teaching often happens in large group settings but more commonly in one-on-one visits. As I speak with clients, prospective clients, and random people who stop to ask me a financial question, I have found that in listening to their challenges, definite patterns emerge. Everyone is different in their specific needs and wants, yet most struggle with very similar problems. Over the years and the thousands of meetings, it seems that some financial questions are asked far more often than others. In an attempt to help more people get to the answers more quickly, I have begun to assemble a list of the most common questions I have been asked. I am hoping that in reading this short book you will find questions you too have asked, and perhaps gain some direction in getting to your own personal answers. Please read all the questions even if it isn't specific to your situation as in each answer I may cover other topics of interest to you.

When you have finished, and if you are like me, I am sure you will have other questions I haven't covered. If so, feel free to send them to me. I will do my best to answer them for you. It's the least I can do to somehow payback my mother for all the time and answers she gave to her very inquisitive son.

The Questions:

Question 1

Can I Afford to Retire?

Having a career can be profitable and fulfilling, but work is work and eventually most people look forward to the day when they won't have to show up every morning. They dream about relaxing, doing projects around the house, taking up hobbies and traveling, playing with grandkids and the like. When the time for retirement gets near many begin to feel a little anxious about the whole thing. Change is often uncomfortable, even if it's a good change, and facing the unknown of retirement can be quite unsettling.

It's quite a moment, after a lifetime of imagining retirement, to actually be staring it in the face. As one friend put it, "When I realized I was going to wake up next week and have no more paychecks, ever, and would have to live the rest of my life solely on what I had saved up, I was absolutely terrified." Retirement is viewed as a time when we gain our freedom to do what our career has gotten in the way of us doing. When it gets closer we may start to view retirement as also a time of loss; loss of friendships, productivity, challenge, personal worth and income. The latter being the most frightening.

Thus, one of the more common questions we hear in our office is, "Can I afford to retire?" Asking your financial advisor if you can afford to retire is like asking your travel agent if you can afford to take a vacation. The answer in both cases is a definite, "Yes" but it's the follow-up questions that are the most critical. Everyone can afford to take a vacation as long as the cost of the vacation does not exceed the available resources. When I am asked this retirement question I respond with some questions of my own. #1 – Tell me what retirement looks like to you and I will tell you if you can afford it. #2 – Tell me what resources you have and I will tell you what type of retirement you can likely afford. If the answers to these questions are not acceptable, then the person is left with the option to put off their retirement.

Retirement is a very personal activity. Everyone sees it differently and as you get closer it continues to change from what you once envisioned. I have pondered this question often in my own life as Launa and I have made plans for our future. I am a planner after all so nothing happens without my spreadsheet.

In my youth I worked a summer on the Hawaiian island of Lanai planting pineapples. It was hard and back-breaking work, literally. A pineapple planter spends their entire day walking, bent fully over, digging pineapple crowns into the ground one at a time. Despite the difficulty of it, I was grateful for the potential income the work would produce because I was paid based on how many I planted. Having always had a desire for the freedom money brings, I didn't mind working hard if it meant a profitable summer. I will say though, that there were many days in those dirty fields with the heat searing my back that I found myself planning for the nice desk job I would one day have. I was certain that if I did well enough I could retire to one of those nice Hawaiian beaches by my 30th birthday.

Like many of my ambitious Baby-boomer generation, when I reached 30 my retirement plan moved back to age 40 and when I turned 40, well, I just had too much going on with my growing family to even consider it. Apart from that, I had moved from the stressful physical work of planting pineapple to the enjoyable occupation of helping other people reach their own retirement goals. In my 40's I was enjoying my work so much I began to think I may never choose to retire.

It was during this time that I decided it would be sad to trade my fulfilling life for the boredom of sitting on a beach. Now as I get close to what many view as an appropriate retirement age, my idea of the approaching "Golden Years" has changed again. I now view my dream retirement as a time to continue being productive at work, but with a more flexible schedule. Having more free time and resources at this stage of life, I think my perfect retirement would include doing some of the things I wasn't able to do while raising our family, while still enjoying continuing to work, albeit at a slower pace.

What does retirement look like to you? Write it down on a piece of paper. Do this even if you are younger. The time to ask if you can afford to retire is not when you are 65, but much younger. Ask the question often and adjust your plans as your dream changes. As you consider your options, write down a list of the resources you have available to pay for it, or that you plan to have. With that information in hand, you can visit with a qualified CFP® professional who will be happy to help you decide if it's possible, or if you are on track.

If you find the numbers will not support your dream, then you will have some choices to make. You may decide to put off retiring for a bit while you build resources, or you may choose to accept a more modest retirement. One important piece of the math puzzle that is commonly overlooked is the double benefit you will get for every extra year you spend on the job. You will have one more year to save money, while being left with one less year of retirement that those savings will need to pay for. We have seen many retirement plans look much better by the individual just choosing to add another year or two to their career.

A third question to consider is, do you really want to retire? We work every day with retired people and I have found that many don't like it as much as they expected to. Several find themselves wishing they would have put it off at least a little longer. A few generations ago, retirement was largely unheard of and it was what happened only if you absolutely were no longer capable of working. Today, with advancement in medicine, many people who retire in their 60's will have 30 or even 40 years left to live. That's a very long time if you don't have something productive to do.

There are as many ways to retire as there are retirees and there is no real rule for how or when it needs to happen. For some that may mean moving into retirement slowly over a period of time. For others it could be putting off the decision completely for a year or two. We also have several people we work with who, like me, have chosen to put off retirement until it is forced upon them. Years ago, we had a lovely lady in our Las Vegas office who spent her lifetime as a showgirl. She loved her work and loved the people she worked with. The thought of retirement felt lonely to her so she continued dancing and performing until her health finally forced her to quit, at age 77. The point is, don't let an arbitrary age define when you need to retire.

Finally, many believe the only job of a financial advisor is to help you make money in the stock and investment markets. That is certainly important but a good advisor will do far more than that. Money really has no value until it is spent. Even if you had a billion dollars in your retirement account, that money is just a number until you convert it to a tangible use. Any part of it that you leave behind when you die has zero value to you personally, but of course has potential value to your beneficiaries. As financial advisors we help people save money, but we also advise on ways to enjoy it. We help people know that it's ok to enjoy the fruits of their labors. It is an irony of life that those who are the best at investing and saving money, seem to have the most difficult time spending it in retirement. A good advisor will help you find the balance so that you can enjoy whatever retirement seems best to you.

In all my years of working with people as their financial advisor, there have been those who had far more than they could ever spend and there have been others who lived on tight budgets until their last breath. In every case we continuously monitor and adjust their plans as needed so that they can get to the end of their life without running out of money. Over the years of our relationship, we have numerous discussions about their wants, needs and resources and then I encourage them to invest and spend money within the parameters that would allow them to successfully live their lives without running out. Thus, once the decision is made to retire, advisor and client work together to see that it happens as planned.

Question 2

How Can I Best Leave Money to My Kids?

This may be right near the top of our most commonly asked questions. I am speaking mostly here to people who are parents. They spend their lives managing their money wisely and doing their best to use it for the benefit of their children, being careful not to do too much. They want their kids to learn to be responsible. Yet death will come to the parents and when it does, they worry how the children will handle any inheritance left behind. I know people think about this a lot because they often change their estate plans many times throughout their lives as a result of their concern. After going through the process of transferring assets to heirs hundreds of times, I have a few thoughts on the matter I'd like to share.

I remember the very first time I held a five-dollar bill of my own. I earned it by working Saturdays at my dad's machine shop. When I got the job, which paid a whopping 50 cents an hour, I dreamed of the candy I would buy when payday came. But as I sat on my bed that day looking at the bill, turning it over and over and seeing those amazing big number 5's on it, I suddenly had a difficult time deciding what to do with it. It was no longer just money waiting to be spent, but it was a valuable representation of long hours of work. Work, that would have been wasted if I wasted the money.

That moment in time is fixed in my memory and was one that played a key role in the way I viewed money throughout my life. By the way, I chose not to buy any candy, but I did spend 75 cents on a very high-end half gallon of chocolate chip ice cream. I kept that special treat in the garage freezer for almost a month, eating it one small spoonful at a time. That money was difficult to earn and I wanted to appreciate every moment of spending it. Learning to respect the value of hard-earned money was a valuable life lesson that my parents gave me many opportunities to re-learn.

One day at Wyson Financial we received a call from the child of one of our long-time clients. We had worked with the client for many years and had a very close relationship. This couple had lived a normal middle-class life, spending wisely and faithfully saving a portion of their monthly income so that their money might last throughout their retirement. As with many of our clients, their income throughout life was moderate, yet the nest egg at the end had grown quite large. They understood and applied basic financial principals and were reaping the rewards in their retirement. We knew they had a single child, a son, but we were also aware their relationship with him was strained. Still, they loved him and listed him as their only heir, asking us often to do what we could to help him manage his inheritance wisely after they were gone.

The phone call was very short and amounted to the man informing us that his last remaining parent had passed away the night before. He promptly asked, "Did my parents leave me any money?" After verifying his identity, we confirmed that they had quite a substantial account and he was listed as the only beneficiary. He simply said, "Sell everything and send it to me." As with most accounts, his parents held short-term and long-term investments. As markets can be volatile and some investments have a time commitment, it's rarely a good idea to just liquidate an account all at once. As we started to explain this he cut us off and said, "I don't care about that. Just cash it out and send it." The tone of the call, literally hours after his parent's death, was disturbing.

This was an unusual experience but not altogether unheard of. Most heirs are more respectful and, even if they are excited to be getting an inheritance, they don't make it so obvious. Still, we see many situations where, as the weeks pass by, heirs often reveal their true colors and behave in a way that would likely sadden their parents. Money can do that to people. Seeing the transfer of assets between generations play out over and over again, has led us to advise our clients to seriously consider the process by which they intend to leave money behind. There are certainly children and other heirs who are well prepared intellectually and emotionally to be given a substantial amount of money, while many others are not.

My experiences have taught me that when you work for money and when you sacrifice to save your money, you have a much greater respect for it. You tend to be more cautious about how you invest and spend it. On the other hand, it is often the case that heirs who are not financially sound themselves, can be very quick to demand their share and even quicker to spend it. Many studies have shown that the average inheritance is spent in less than a year.

If your estate plans include "leaving a little something" for your kids, consider that your good financial example and some well-timed lessons can be much better than a big check. One of the best things my parents did for me financially was to give me the chance to earn that $5 bill, and many more, by providing opportunities for hard, honest work. Those lessons have blessed my entire life far more than any money they might have left.

But what about those children who never had a chance to learn, or who chose not to? Aging parents are often stuck in a difficult situation. As good parents they want to bless the lives of their children by leaving a little something behind. They want to know their kids and grandkids will have sufficient for their needs and emergencies and even some pleasures, but they don't want the money to make the heirs lazy or selfish. They also don't want them to waste the money. Even worse, I have seen heirs buy bigger homes and nicer cars and toys, then when the money is spent they cannot afford to maintain those items and they find themselves worse off financially than before the inheritance. So what is to be done? Money is a great tool but it can also be a curse.

Most people don't think about it but the largest single financial transaction of your life will quite possibly be the one you make on the day you die. On that day you instantly transfer your entire accumulated net worth, to someone else. It is amazing therefore, how little thought some people put into that moment. Parents may spend more time planning a child's birthday gift than an inheritance. Some laughingly say, "It will be my kids' problem when I die." Unfortunately, that is often the case.

Whether your assets are large or small, figuring out how to leave them to an heir can be a challenge. Every situation is unique and there are no perfect answers. This is evident in my own life as I review my personal estate plan several times a year. In my career I've seen the bad effects of too many poor decisions, or worse, too many neglected decisions regarding estate planning. Here are a few key points worth considering.

I believe there are basically two types of heirs: those who are good with money and those who are not. The first group generally does not need your money, and the second group will not know what to do with it. Group one will likely add your kind gift to their own nest egg and move forward in life as they otherwise would have. Group two may think they have won the lottery and go on a spending spree, winding up with expensive items to care for, leaving them worse off than before the inheritance. As you plan your inheritance options with your CFP®, I suggest focusing largely on the effect the money will have on group two.

Money can be left to heirs as a lump sum, or in a series of payments. My personal preference for most is to stretch out the inheritance over time, at least a part of it. Payments that last a lifetime can have a more positive effect than a chunk of money that is quickly spent. Even if it's a small amount, it can make a difference. Stretching out payments has the added benefit of continually reminding your heirs how much they are loved. I have wealthy clients who do not need the monthly checks they receive from their deceased parents' estate, but when they arrive, they treasure them.

In one experience a couple chose, instead of a single lump sum, to leave their 3 children regular payments for the rest of their lives. They knew their children were not prepared for a large sum of money so we arranged (and there are several ways to do this) for a monthly check to go to each child until the end of their own lives. I remember clearly when the three heirs sat in my conference room to work out the distribution of the estate. I started by telling them, "I have good news and bad news for you today. The good news is your share of the estate is going to be about double what you expected." Big smiles came to all their faces. "The bad news is that it will take you the rest of your lives to receive it all." As their smiles disappeared I explained to them the details of the payments they would be receiving. No, they were not happy. I'm sure they already had the new car and maybe a boat picked out. But I explained to them how much their parents loved them and wanted to leave a gift that would last a lifetime.

It was about three years later that one of the children called to tell me how much they had come to appreciate that monthly check from their parents' estate. Admitting he was angry at first, the child confessed that he would have in fact wasted the money if given it all at once, but every month now when that check arrives he is grateful for the foresight of his parents. This phone call was a treasure to me and had the parents still been alive to hear it, would have been a treasure to them as well.

Another important aspect of estate planning is the process by which you pass on financial knowledge to your heirs so they are better prepared to receive an inheritance. I love to see my clients use retirement funds to spend on and with their children and grandchildren while they, the parents, are still living. Doing so builds valuable memories and has the added benefit of teaching about the value of saving, growing and using money wisely. I have found that heirs who have shared in the benefits of wise money management, tend to be better money managers themselves.

Finally, just because you have it doesn't mean your kids should inherit it. If you love them, don't leave an heir more money than they can wisely handle. You make these types of judgment calls every day as a parent and grandparent. Don't abdicate that responsibility when the biggest financial day of your life arrives. There are many wonderful ways to leave behind a financial legacy when you die. No one answer is right for everyone so talk to a good financial advisor who has been through this many times with other clients and can show you several options that have worked well. It will likely be your biggest financial day so make it count.

Question 3

What Do You Charge?

A couple stopped by one day in search of a new financial advisor. They had visited with several and had assembled a spreadsheet listing, among other factors, the fees each one quoted. The fees, based on the account size, ranged from .8 to 1.8% of the account value per year. In our discussion it was clear they were giving a heavy weighting to the fees since they said they definitely would not be using the person who quoted them 1.8%.

I asked this couple what it was that had brought them to my office that day and they responded that they had suffered uncomfortable losses in the markets over the past couple of years and they were hoping a different advisor might do better for them. I asked them to consider a question as we proceeded with our discussion. I said, "You seem very focused on what your next advisor will charge you, and that is a legitimate question. But given your past losses wouldn't it make more sense to consider not what your advisor costs, but rather what your advisor is worth?" Then I shared the following story:

One year I wanted to do something really special for Launa's birthday so I commissioned a nationally renowned artist to do a watercolor painting of her in our home. I had paid a street painter years before while visiting Italy to do a charcoal sketch of Launa, and we both loved it so much that I felt she would treasure even more a portrait done on a much

15

higher level. The street painter, in the 20 minutes he had, did a great job and created a wonderful memory. But the professional artist, who spent long hours in our house over a couple of days created a cherished heirloom that captured the beauty of my wonderful wife, sitting at her piano that she loves so much. It will be a permanent treasure for our family and our posterity.

The painters had different skills and the paintings had different purposes. One was a fun memory of a great vacation. The other was designed to capture, for generations to come, Launa's personality, her beauty and her passion for music. When the professional artist initially quoted me the price my first thought was that it was pretty high. When she delivered the finished work I realized it wasn't those hours I was paying for, but her lifetime of training and experience that made those hours so valuable.

When I gave Launa the finished work she asked how much I had paid for it. I responded I paid as much as I needed to. I might note at this point that these many years later the professional work is proudly hanging in a prominent place in our living room, while I do not know where the drawing done by the street artist is.

The couple who came to my office looking for a new advisor because their account had performed so poorly, were overly focused on what they would be charged rather than the quality of the service they would be getting. And what is it that makes a good financial advisor? Proper financial planning takes into account personal preferences, risk tolerances, goals, lifestyles and more. A good advisor applies as much art as science in helping a family reach their goals. Considering how much to pay for professional financial advice is like deciding how much to pay for an artist. In either case, try to never overpay, but in my experience, underpaying is almost always worse.

All this is not to imply that good financial advisors are expensive. In fact, most of the best ones I know are priced very competitively. More importantly, investors must remember that the biggest price they often pay is the price of poor advice. Or even worse, the cost of no advice. In several large studies it has been determined that having a good financial advisor can add up to 4% annually to your net returns, versus managing your portfolio on your own[1]. That is a significant number when spread over a lifetime. What is interesting about these studies is that the researchers found it wasn't necessarily stock picking that made the difference. Much of the extra gains came from the advice advisors were giving that kept their clients from jumping in and out of investments at the wrong time. They also helped manage contributions and withdrawals in an efficient manner known as sequencing, further adding to their worth. In short, researchers found that a good financial advisor was worth more than what most were charging.

When shopping for an advisor I recommend focusing on the quality of the advice and associated service. Only after you find a good fit, then talk about price and make sure that it is reasonable and competitive.

[1]Envestnet, Capital Sigma, The Advisor Advantage (estimates advisor adds an average of 3% per year); Russell Investments 2019 Value of a Financial Advisor (estimates advisor adds more than 4% per year); Vanguard, Quantifying Vanguard Advisor's Alpha® 2019, (estimates lifetime value add at an average of 3% annually)

Question 4

How Would You Invest $100,000?

I'm not joking about this one. We get this question all the time, and it usually comes from a random person who just found out I am a financial advisor.

When someone learns that the person they just met is a doctor, it is not uncommon for them to roll up their sleeve and say, "Well hey doc, since you're here can you take a quick look at this thing?" All doctors reading this know exactly what I'm talking about. As a financial advisor I often run into the same situation with the question being some form of, "Hey, since you are the expert, suppose I gave you $100,000 to invest. What would you do with it?"

Most doctors answer the question by suggesting the individual make an appointment to see them in their office. They understand that the proper practice of medicine involves understanding all the facts. I usually answer the question by turning it around and asking the person about their career. If he says he is an architect I would reply, "That's wonderful, we have been thinking of building a new house. If I had you design it what would it look like?" He would usually laugh a little and reply that it would be impossible to answer such a question without a lengthy discussion about my family, our lifestyle, budget, wants and needs. He would add that he often spends weeks with people methodically working through many questions before he even begins to put anything down on paper.

If by this point in the conversation he hasn't caught on, I will generally say, "Well then you understand why I can't recommend how to invest your money when I just barely met you."

I have been present when other financial advisors were asked a similar question and, anxious to appear intelligent, answered it in great detail. These situations took me back to when I was first learning the business in my youth and my dad warned me to beware of the "30 second expert." There are few things in life more critical than good management of financial resources. The success and very survival of businesses, families, marriages and individuals depends upon it. Like designing a home, solving a medical issue, or creating a great work of art, it takes time.

On a personal level we all need to recognize the risk of becoming our own 30 second expert. I know many investors who after reading an article or a social media post rush to buy some investment. For fear of missing out they move too quickly before doing proper research. Rarely do such rash decisions turn out well. I remind people that opportunities for investing always exist so there is rarely a need to rush into anything.

If you are tempted to invest without proper thought, take a deep breath and slow down. Likewise, offering you advice on how you should invest without thoroughly understanding your situation is clear evidence an advisor is not qualified to be giving financial advice. Or, they are one of those advisors who gives the same advice to everyone, which is even more dangerous. In either case you should avoid these types, seeking instead an advisor who values their advice enough to not give it until they know enough about you to offer a truly professional opinion.

Question 5

Isn't the Stock Market Just a Big Casino?

I have always been very optimistic when it comes to our nation and its future. During a major economic downturn, I taught a series of seminars entitled "A Case for Optimism" in which I demonstrated the reasons why the naysayers had it wrong. Many who attended those seminars were sincerely thankful for my perspective. I basically taught that there are many investment sectors of our economy that we can choose to invest in. We have large cap, small and mid-cap, value and growth, real estate etc., and all of them have one thing in common. They all have positive returns over time. If you take the biggest financial disasters in our history such as the great depression, WW1, WW2, interest rates near 20% in the early 80's, the dot.com crash, the 911 attack, the great recession of 2008 and the worldwide pandemic, in every single situation the stock market recovered and went on to hit new highs. That is a 100% success rate[1]. It's quite a remarkable record if you look at it.

Despite the markets' long-term record, there will always be those who are negative. There will always be those who are pessimistic and who predict failure for our country, our economy, and our stock market. Some are negative because they make money with negativity and others truly believe that the stock market is just one big casino with the odds mostly stacked against the average investor.

When I hear naysayers putting down the stock market by comparing it to a casino, I realize I am listening to someone who likely doesn't understand either. Or perhaps worse, it is someone who has a competing product to sell and preaching fear brings in the money. In either case I have somewhat of a unique understanding of how casinos work. I spent some of the best years of my life living in Las Vegas at a time when it was a relatively small town. Our family lived near downtown Vegas and my brother and I used to regularly ride our bicycles up and down Fremont Street and the Strip, hopping in pools along the way to escape the searing Vegas heat. Yes, this was a few years ago.

As a bit of a math prodigy, while in high school I was once hired by a professional gambler to analyze a few systems he had developed for beating the casinos. As a simple description of my job, he would give me his betting strategy and have me apply it to a 36-hour history he had compiled of rolls of the dice at a craps table. I would compare the outcomes to the imaginary dollars my client might bet, and determine how much he would have won or lost. This was all before computers or even electronic calculators, so I did the math in my head. For my work I was paid a whopping $10 an hour, which was huge in those days.

During the time of my employment I learned a lot about the gambling process and, what I now know is called the "Law of Large Numbers (LLN)." This law states that as the sample size increases, the actual results come closer to the expected averages. An example would be tossing a penny. The expected results would be 50% heads and 50% tails but it's very possible to toss it 10 times and come up with a 70% heads, or more. However, if you tossed the penny a billion times the distribution of the results would come to a statistical 50/50 tie every time. The LLN is extremely dependable.

It is the same law that assures life insurance companies will always come out ahead if they have enough customers, the lottery will always make money for the government and a casino will ultimately win no matter how small of an advantage they have. So a casino gambler, as I demonstrated to my employer, will always eventually lose if he plays long enough because he receives nothing of value in return for his investment, and he is betting against natural law. This law was also taught to me some years later when I took a job working for one of Las Vegas' largest Casino hotels, the original Hilton, as I worked my way through college.

At that time the hotel invented a concept known as Megabucks. They set up a bank of slot machines that took $1 coins, which was unheard of at the time. The machines surrounded a display that offered a $250,000 jackpot, also unheard of at the time. The marketing around Megabucks brought in gamblers from near and far much the way the super Lotteries do today. During the first year of the promotion it seems to me that they paid out the jackpot about 20 times. I remember one day talking to the hotel manager while working my shift and commenting about the jackpot being hit the night before. I said something to the effect of, "I bet you hate it when that happens." He laughed and then told me that every time the jackpot was hit they would make a big deal about it to the news, and that resulted in the machines being packed with gamblers for many weeks to come. "I love it when someone wins," he said, "because the ultimate winner is always the house."

Casinos understand the LLN which is why they always win. Yes, on occasion an individual player may hit the jackpot and in so doing declare that they had "beaten the odds," but this is not actually true. The odds, which are based on the LLN, are never beaten. They always win because the odds are not based on a single player, but on the totality of players and dollars that change hands over a large sample, or a long period of time. To a casino, that is all that matters.

Now consider what happens with an investment in the stock market. First, unlike gamblers, a wise investor receives something of value in return for their investment. They are given ownership in a company, or even hundreds of companies, that produce goods and services that the world needs and wants. In the short term those investments can be volatile for a number of reasons, but in the long term the volatility gives way to the potential profits and growth of the companies owned. Long term investors recognize economic cycles for what they are and invest appropriately, neither getting too excited when things go up, nor too discouraged when they go down. Investments in businesses that produce products of value are investments in the future of our nation and growing nations around the world. Based on the long-term record of the U.S. stock markets, the investors actually have the LLN working in their favor. The longer they invest, the more likely they are to receive the increasing returns of the growing markets. If they invest with discipline and enough time the so-far perfect record of recovery of the US stock market plays to their great advantage. Just as it can be said that in Vegas the house always eventually wins, it can also be said that based on the history of the stock market, investors win because, in the stock market, investors *are* the house.

For over 200 years the US stock market has shown to be a tremendous machine for wealth creation. In the simplest sense, it represents the hopes and hard work of the American people and, in my opinion, those who bet against it may be the true gamblers. Conversely, those who have taken a well-thought-out approach to investing in a variety of stocks, have a very strong historical record on their side. Math and the LLN are powerful tools and with proper guidance they can be used to greatly increase the opportunity for investing success.

There are two cautions I must share at this point. The first comes from a man I met in 2015. He came into our office after reading one of my newspaper columns. He had about $3 million dollars, 100% of which was sitting in his bank account. I asked him why it was there. He said it was because when the stock market crashed in 2008 he lost $400,000 so he pulled all his money out (by the way, he was not the only one who reacted in that way at the time). As he told me this, I was thinking that taking his money out of the stock market after a big crash would be akin to the Hilton casino closing its doors after a slot player hit a jackpot. I made the observation, "You did not lose your $400,000 because of the crash of '08. You lost that money because of *your* response to it."

As the meeting progressed, we went over the man's lifetime of investing and discovered that the money he thought he had "lost" in 2008 was actually only a small portion of what the same stock market had made for him in the many years prior. The market was not losing him money but merely averaging out his total returns. Then I pointed out the painful truth, which he already knew. I estimated, based on what he had owned in 2008, how much more than $3 million he would have had right then had he just left it alone. His losses in 2008 would have been dwarfed by the huge market recovery that took place from 2009-2015. While his money sat earning next to nothing in the bank for 7 years, the stock market and the LLN took over and made money for those people who let it work its magic. This really isn't magic at all. It's just math. You have to love math don't you? It never lets you down.[2]

The second caution is to remember that though the stock market is not a casino, there are investors who choose to treat it as such. Buying and selling based on short term trends or getting involved in high-risk strategies is a whole different world than long-term investing and negates the value of the LLN because they do not give it sufficient time to function. If that is how you choose to use the stock market, in my opinion you might as well book yourself a seat at a crap table in Vegas. At least as you are losing your money the casino might offer you a few complimentary drinks or show tickets to help ease your suffering.

Of course, when it comes to investing, past performance is not a guarantee of future results, but it would be hard to ignore the remarkable 200-year history of the US stock market when making decisions with your investable dollars.

[1]Looking at the stock market in its entirety, not any stock individually.[2] Of course the stock market is not a direct correlation to numerical averages, casino games or tossing coins. There are always anomalies that cannot be accounted for including the human factor. There is always risk. But I use this as an example that the history of the stock market as a whole is remarkable and worth considering. Those who compare a balanced and wise stock portfolio to casino gambling are making a demonstrably false comparison.

Question 6

Should I buy an Annuity?

It would be difficult to find a financial product surrounded in more debate and controversy than annuities. In my experience there doesn't seem to be very much middle ground. People seem to love them or hate them. I choose to approach annuities the way I approach just about everything in the financial world. I recognize that like tools in my garage, when I have a job to do I choose the tool suited for the job. I will admit there have been times, more common in my youth, when I couldn't find the correct tool, so I just had to make do. Sometimes you can get away with it - like when I use the handle of a big screwdriver to pound a small nail when a hammer isn't close by. At other times, using the wrong tool is just plain ineffective, or even damaging. I can be pretty creative with tools but ultimately, there is nothing quite like having exactly what you need for the job at hand.

I have never personally owned an annuity, not because I don't like them but rather because I have not yet had a personal need for one. But I have helped clients use annuities to solve specific financial needs. At the same time, I have discouraged others from using annuities because I felt a different option (or tool) was a better solution. As an example, I was recently trying to fix a problem with a phillips screwdriver when a flathead was needed. The experience was frustrating, but it wasn't the screwdriver's fault.

I have counselled many individuals who had purchased an annuity elsewhere and came to realize it was not a good fit for them. In those situations, the exit options may be limited and costly, so I always advise those who decide to use an annuity to solve a financial problem to do their careful due diligence first. My point is, when people have issues with annuities, it has been my experience that it is not usually the annuity's fault but the improper placement of it.

In order to decide if an annuity is right for you, let's first review the nature of these products as they come in several sizes with a vast array of options (*a brief word of caution. The next couple of pages could get a bit dry. If you aren't particularly interested in learning about the workings of annuities, feel free to skip to question 7*).

What is an Annuity? At their foundation, an annuity is a life insurance product. They are issued by insurance companies and are required to have some insurance aspect. This means the issuer (insurance company) must tie the product to a person's life (the annuitant) and the insurer must take risk as it relates to that person. Generally, that risk is associated with how long a person might live, and what guaranteed commitments the insurer has in relation to their lifespan.

Fees –Issuers charge fees to cover such things as the risk that the annuitant might die too soon or live too long, potential market risks that they must absorb, paying commissions to the selling agent, and covering the ongoing costs of administering the annuity. They also need to make a profit.

These fees will vary greatly with the type of annuity and should be thoroughly understood when a potential buyer compares them to other products. Annuity fees are often embedded in the product and may be difficult to assess. Salespeople sometimes advertise annuities as having no fees, which is misleading. If the insurer is paying a cost, including a high commission, those costs are ultimately born by the customer regardless of how they are paid.

Guarantees – A main attraction of annuities is the guarantee of principal or income or both. Since the guarantee comes from the insurance company, their financial strength is very important. Some states offer minimal guarantees for certain annuities, but most make it illegal for a salesperson to use state guarantees in their marketing.

Types of Annuities – Annuities generally have an accumulation phase and a distribution phase. The various types affect how these two phases operate.

Fixed Annuity – These have fixed rates of return during accumulation, and then guaranteed payout amounts during distribution. They are the easiest to understand as their terms are specifically spelled out. An example would be a 10-year certain annuity that is guaranteed to pay 5% per year for 10 years, period. Another would be a life annuity that pays a fixed monthly payment for as long as person lives. In the latter case the amount of the payout will be determined by the lifespan of the annuitant.

Variable Annuity - In this product the value is invested in various market products like mutual funds, ETFs, bond funds etc. The growth, or shrinkage, of the account value will depend upon the returns of the underlying investments. You can lose money in this type of annuity as it is market based. There will often be some guarantees of minimum returns or payouts based on too many factors to list here. Purchasers should carefully scrutinize these guarantees to see if they make sense for them. Remember that market investments charge internal fees, and the insurer charges their own fees so the costs associated with a variable annuity will most likely be higher than if a person bought the same investments directly outside of the annuity.

Fixed Indexed Annuity - These are perhaps the most confusing of the group, and potentially the most subject to misrepresentation. These are one of the leading sources of complaints to regulators as it relates to annuities due to their complexity and the sometimes-aggressive efforts of salespeople to sell them. An indexed annuity ties itself to certain market indexes, for example the S&P 500, and offers a portion of the growth of that index without any risk to the downside. On the face of it they sound like the perfect investment. Who wouldn't want stock market growth without risk? But the challenge comes in the details. Since insurers must cover their risks, owners of these annuities only receive a "portion" of the market upside in exchange for no risk to principal. How this portion is calculated can be very confusing, even for the people who sell them. Purchasers are advised to get a second opinion on these products from someone who understands the methods for crediting gains.

A major caveat of Indexed annuities is that many of them, or even most of them, allow the insurer to change the terms of the crediting method each year on the anniversary. If the insurer reduces the potential payout on an anniversary, the annuity owner may get stuck with a product that is no longer suitable for them. Surrender penalties often make it unfeasible to walk away. Our advice is to not buy an indexed annuity unless you fully understand how and when the issuer can change the crediting methods, and what that may mean to you. We have seen many sales agents give overly optimistic estimates of the potential returns of indexed annuities using historical numbers and crediting methods that may not apply in the future.

Annuitization – this is the option to tell the insurer that you want to turn on a fixed stream of income. So rather than continuing to receive the growth of the annuity, you decide you want monthly or annual payments that are fixed in some fashion and guaranteed for a fixed period of years or the rest of your life. If for the rest of your life it is called a "life annuity" and the insurer assumes the risk of paying you for as long as you live no matter how long that may be. Of course, if your life is unusually shortened, your returns will be much less. This can be a great benefit because it works much like a guaranteed pension. The downside is that the guaranteed amount may not keep up with inflation or other potential investments, but it is guaranteed and so there can be a measure of peace for those who prefer that.

Taxation of Annuities - Annuities may have tax benefits for some as they generally allow growth to be tax-deferred. However, when money is withdrawn it is taxed at regular income rates, not as long-term capital gains. This same method applies to heirs who will not receive a step-up in basis as currently exists with many other investments. Taxation is a complicated issue and should be reviewed with your qualified tax advisor before purchasing an annuity. Also, tax benefits are lost if the annuity is bought within a Qualified (IRA) type of account.

Situations where an annuity might make sense:

- You are more concerned with safety of principle than rate of return

- A fixed income for life is important enough that you are willing to sacrifice liquidity and potential higher returns in exchange for stability, accepting that inflation may be your greatest risk.

-Heirs are often unprepared to handle large inheritances. Leaving them a portion as a lifetime annuity payment is one way to guarantee their inheritance will never run out. In this situation the rate of return takes a backseat to a desire to give your heirs the gift that will last a lifetime. We consider this one of the best uses of annuities.

-If you want to participate in a portion of the stock market returns without risk to principal, accepting that crediting methods may potentially make this method even less profitable than other guaranteed and potentially more liquid options.

Annuities can be complex products that are often over-simplified by salespeople. Internal fees can be high and salespeople can be paid high commissions to sell them. Even if you don't pay the commission directly, it ultimately comes from your money and will affect your results. One of the main reasons for high surrender penalties in many annuities is to allow the insurer to recoup the selling commission if you should cancel the policy early.

Annuities are guaranteed products with a life insurance feature and may also have an investment option. They can do things no other assets can do and if you need those benefits they are worth a look. If you do not need the life insurance aspect you may want to consider other options.

A Final Note. One of the main ways to market annuities is through so-called free dinner seminars. These meetings are usually advertised as educational only but the high cost of putting on these events puts a high amount of pressure on salespeople to sell the products. Regulators report that free dinner annuity sales are a major source of investor complaints. If you believe an annuity may be for you, our advice is to visit with your trusted financial advisor rather than a stranger offering you free food. Otherwise, it may turn out to be the most expensive free meal you ever had.

Is an annuity for you? It may be. They have many proper and good uses, but my opinion is that they are used more often than they should be. Consulting with a CFP® professional would be a good first step in assessing if these products are suitable for you.

If you have an annuity and want to get out of it, do not do so without having a qualified advisor do a cost versus benefits assessment so that you may make an informed decision. As a general rule you should not buy an annuity unless you are prepared to hold it to full term. Getting out early can be costly and though sometimes necessary, should be the exception.

Question 7

When Should I Start Social Security?

This question is always a challenging one because the answer is so personal. *When* you decide to retire and begin taking Social Security (SS) will affect the next 30-40 years of your life. And though you can actually change your mind to some degree down the road, most view these as fairly permanent decisions.

There is a factor in the SS decision many do not consider that involves some questions I believe are worth asking. It begins by turning to your own personal SS page on the government website. As I look at my page there is something that stands out to me. There is a graph that shows what my payments will be, based on the date I retire. There are three key dates on that graph. The first is age 62 which is the earliest you can take SS under normal circumstances. The second is the full retirement age, which is about 5 years later depending on the year of your birth. The final number is age 70. The graph shows the expected amount (there is no guarantee until you actually claim it) that would be received at those three ages. Of course, the longer you wait to start the benefits, the higher the expected payment goes. But here is what caught my eye. The difference between age 62 and age 70 was about a 75% increase, and the way the graph lays it out seems to be designed to magnify that increase. In other words, I got the feeling while looking at the graph that it was designed to encourage me to wait so that I can receive higher payments. In fact, in several areas of the government website there are references to how much more a person can be paid if they wait, with payments going up for every month of delay. At one spot the site posted in bold letters that delaying your Social Security payments would be a great way to "Juice Your Payout." It seemed odd that the Social Security department would try to get people to choose an option that would end up costing the government more money.

Ronald Reagan cynically quipped, "I'm from the government and I'm here to help." With that in mind I wondered, what is the truth behind waiting or not waiting to collect social security? The government is the debtor in this situation and it's in a debtor's best interest to get the best deal for themselves. So, with this in mind I decided to look deeper into the implied claim that, "If you wait to take SS, you will be paid more money." I suspected the government's advice may be tainted given its clear conflict of interest in the matter.

Let me illustrate the challenge of deciding when to start your social security payments with a totally fictitious example of two friends, Slim and Biff, who were both born on the same day, and worked their entire lives at the same factory for the same wage. In my fictitious example, I will make up the numbers to illustrate a point and will leave out any cost-of-living increases, assuming the effect would be the same for either party (You may need to read this story a couple of times with pencil in hand to scratch notes, but it will be worth it).

When the two friends turned 62, they both retired from work but debated about when to take SS benefits. The amount would be $1,500 but if they waited until age 70 it was estimated to be $2,600, or about 75% more. Slim wanted to start payments right away, but Biff was tempted by the larger number and opted to put off his benefits until age 70.

So Slim started receiving his $1,500 check and enjoyed spending his extra cash for 8 years while his friend received no SS benefits. Finally on the friends' 70th birthdays, Biff's payments began and he was now proudly receiving $2,600 each month (remember I am leaving out cost of living increases for simplicity). Biff was pretty happy with his new income which was a full $1,100 a month more than his friend. However, during the prior 8 years the payments to Slim had totaled a whopping $144,000. Based on these numbers, even with his higher pay it would take Biff 131 months before he would break even with Slims total benefits. They would be nearly 81 years old. After that age, Biff's accumulated income would continue to surpass his friend's.

When people compare taking early versus taking late, it's easy to do the math that this story lays out. But what the math overlooks is the one glaring challenge in a real-life situation. If anytime between ages 62 and 80 the men died, Slim would have come out ahead. If Biff dies before age 70 he gets nothing for his many years of contributing to the system. Up until age 81 he would still receive less than his friend. So, the real question of when to take benefits revolves around the more critical question, "When are you going to die?" If you have longevity in your family, it may make sense to wait... but does it really? There is still more to this decision.

What I often point out to our clients is that after age 80 life tends to slow down for most people (please don't send me nasty emails). I know there are many very active octogenarians out there but clearly our activity level slows down significantly as we age. Simply put, for most people, taking benefits early gives you additional spendable income during the years when you may be more likely to enjoy it.

There are many more factors at play in this equation. If your retirement funds outside of social security are a bit thin, it may be best to keep working a few more years and get that benefit higher. There are other personal reasons to wait or not wait which is why each person needs to do an individualized assessment. But generally speaking, I find two compelling reasons for taking it early. First, you may not live as long as you expect so you might as well start those payments early. Second, your lifestyle in early retirement may benefit more from some extra spending money than your lifestyle in later retirement.

Before concluding let me add one more twist to the story of the two friends. Let's assume that Slim still takes his SS at retirement with a payment of $1,500, but rather than spending it he invests it all in a modest investment account that hypothetically earns 6% per year. When the two friends reach age 70 Biff starts his SS benefits, collecting $2,600 a month. Slim decides to stop saving and start spending so he begins drawing out his $1,500 monthly check. In order to stay even with his friend, he pulls $1100 monthly from his SS investment account that he has been saving. Slim's investment account, at 6% hypothetical return, would have grown to $186,664. Let's pause here for a moment and realize if both men die together at age 70, Biff will have received no benefit at all from SS while Slim will at least leave that big pot of money he has been saving up for 8 years to his heirs. That is significant. What is also significant is that under this scenario it will be 31 years before Slim's investment account runs out. Slim would be 101 years old.

With this very simplified example, and as I said, leaving out inflation adjustments which could be assumed would be equal to both men, it seems that in most situations there is a strong and compelling reason to consider taking SS earlier rather than later. According to the SS website, about 12% of 62-year-olds will not make it to age 70 and about 74% will not reach age 90. When considering if you should take benefits early or late you might consider the words of Clint Eastwood, "Do you feel lucky?"

Many advisors and even the SS department promote the idea that the longer you wait, the more you will get; but that only applies if you live long enough and, as you can see, you have to live quite a while. It also depends on when the money would be of best use to you. These are personal decisions. I just want to give you a perspective on it that is often overlooked. The government seems to prefer that you wait. That is a key to me that it may not be in your best interests.

Question 8

Where Can I Invest Without Risk?

Years ago we had several people coming to our Las Vegas office to ask about investing in second trust deeds. Local developers who were unable to acquire traditional loans were offering investors interest rates in the mid-teens at a time when normal commercial loans were going for about half that. When these potential investors asked my opinion, I would respond with the following question: "Why do you think the developer is willing to pay you 14% interest?" Then I would answer my own question with, "Because they offered 13% and no one would take them up on it." After adding a little wink, the person would get my point. When someone wants to borrow money or attract investors, they pay as much as they have to but not more than they need to. The more risk involved in the transaction, the more expensive the money will be.

Investing involves risk. If it didn't, it wouldn't be very profitable. It's the risk factor that allows an investor to attempt to match the amount of return they are hoping to obtain with the level of risk they are willing to take. I have read many definitions of what risk is but the very best came from a college professor who taught that "Risk, is the likelihood of disappointment." I love how that makes the process personal. Most people assume that the more risk you take, the more money you can make. This may be true in a sense, but my professor reminded us that as you enter any financial transaction, the higher the risk the more likely you are to be disappointed in the outcome. I advised our Las Vegas friends to not get involved in those second trust deeds.

A person who buys a bank certificate of deposit at 3% will get exactly what they expect. A person who loans money to a developer offering 14% has a good likelihood of not receiving what they expect. As it turns out, many of those developers made the national news when they defaulted on those second trust deeds. Those investors who did not take my advice to avoid that offer were very disappointed in the outcome. Before we leave this story let's remember that even buying a guaranteed bank CD is not without risk, such as inflation, but at least there are no surprises.

When we do annual reviews in our office ~~we~~ have our clients read and then sign a document called our "Annual risk assessment." The document starts off by saying, "If you are interested in risk-free investments, this is not the right place for you. All investments carry at least some risk." I always enjoy the look on people's faces when they first read this. I think they are accustomed to advisors who only talk about the upside, but all investments have a possible downside, and a good client relationship requires that we discuss it. The document then goes on to list some of the potential risks investments may have as follows:

Market Risk – A particular market may move against you (*You own the best oil company in the world but the world price of oil collapses*)

Credit Risk – The entity you invest in may not be able to make its payments to you (*You buy a bond in a strong company but its' fortunes turn south*)

Business Risk – An individual business may not do as well as expected or hoped for (*You invest in a company that is selling a ton of product and a larger competitor enters the market*)

Inflation Risk – Your return on an investment may not keep up with inflation (*You buy a CD at 3% and inflation goes to 5%, meaning you are literally losing 2% per year in buying power*)

Liquidity Risk – You may not be able to sell an investment at a time when you need the money (*You own a good long-term investment but suddenly have a short-term emergency financial need and can't get at your money*)

Social/Political Risk – Unfavorable government actions or social events may cause you to lose value (*You buy stock in a manufacturer of a product that is outlawed or restricted by legislation – or – you own a successful company that gets targeted by customer boycotts*)

Currency Risk – Changing exchange rates among countries may affect your returns (*If you own a company that relies of foreign manufacturing then you can be affected by changes in currency values*)

Investment Manager Risk – Despite best efforts, Investment managers both in-house and 3rd party cannot predict markets nor guarantee the results of their investment decisions.

Other – There are other potential risks to investing that cannot be listed here.

As I was thinking about how inflation has such a huge effect on real rate of return, I had the idea to open google maps and look up the "dream" home my grandparents built in California in 1940. The ocean view house cost them a whopping $8,000. It's value today is listed at around $1.25 million. That wonderful large gain hides the many years their homes' price went down during difficult markets. Volatility is the very nature of investing, but over time that $8000 would have been a marvelous investment. Or would it? I wondered what if my family still owned that home today?

Some quick math shows the annualized return on that $8,000 to be about 6.3% (as of the date of this writing). Since historic inflation is typically about 3.5%, it could be said the home was a good investment because its price, relative to inflation, actually increased. If your investments don't keep up with inflation, even though the dollars may get larger, the value is going down. Imagine if my grandparents instead had invested that $8,000 in something earning only 3%? Their "investment" today would have grown to about $90,000. That's a large "dollar" gain, but they would struggle to buy a house with it.

I share this story because during times of stock market volatility the so-called "safe money" salespeople come out of the woodwork. Offering their "no-risk" investments they play on the fears created by the daily news cycle. They put out claims about their financial skills such as "None of our clients have ever lost a penny in the stock market," of course without pointing out that none of their clients have made a penny in the stock market either. Ironically, when my grandparents sold their dream home it was during a severe downturn in the real estate market. Yet they still made a handsome profit with which they were able to buy their next dream home.

We need to lose the concept of thinking an investment is good just because it doesn't lose you any "dollars." Even increasing in dollars isn't adequate. Investing is about maintaining and increasing "purchasing power," otherwise you are going backwards. In order for me to have the same home my grandparents had, their $8,000 has to become my $1.25 million. Otherwise, I may have increased "dollars" but lost "value." Keeping ahead of inflation in your long-term investments requires taking some risk and dealing with some volatility. There really is no other way. Those who preach "risk-free" investments are at best kidding themselves and at worst, being unfair to the people who trust them. Nothing in life is risk free.

Where can you invest your money safely? There is really no place that is 100% guaranteed. There are investments that guarantee your principal, but as noted above, if inflation erodes its value then what is really guaranteed? If we look back at the history of the human race we can find examples for all kinds of disasters, both natural and man-made. No matter what level of guarantee, I could give you an example of how investing in anything during those times could potentially fail. Even U.S. government insured bonds and notes are backed by "the full faith and credit of the U.S. government" and the financial world considers these to be "risk-free," but there are still scenarios where that backing could fail.

When people think of risk, they usually consider the possibility that they might lose money. But many people overlook perhaps one of the greatest financial risks they face which is the risk of doing nothing, or not doing enough. By my definition, an investment needs to grow, not only in dollar value but it must also increase in real value relative to other assets. If it does not, then even if the principal is guaranteed, inflation will eat away at its buying power, thus, I like to call this "losing money - safely."

I don't want to take more risk than I need to take. But I consider it just as dangerous to take less risk than I need. As an investor, I want to save money and have it grow over the course of my life not only in dollar amount but in real relative value. To do less would be the greatest risk for me because, as my professor taught, if my nest egg is not large enough to fund my retirement, then I truly will be disappointed. That is the real risk I try to help people avoid.

The 9th Question

Every year a company by the name of Dalbar releases an interesting report regarding investor behavior. Their goal is to determine how the accounts of regular investors perform in relation to the markets they invest in. The report focuses on investors in a general mix of US stocks much like you might find in a fund that tries to imitate the S&P 500, or the Down Jones Industrial Average (DOW). Investing takes time and effort and the purpose of the research is to see if that is paying off for investors. The theory is if an investor would do just as well by simply buying and holding a basket of stocks similar to an index like the DOW, then why waste their efforts trying to make their own selections?

According to the Dalbar study, how would you guess the body of average investors do compared to an unmanaged bucket of the general stocks the investor has to choose from? As I have tracked this research over the years I continue to be amazed at the results as it is far different from what I would have expected. I assumed that the results would be similar but that isn't even close. According to Nerd Wallet, the S&P 500 averaged a bit more that 9% annually over the 30 years ending Dec 31, 2023. An investor would have to do better than that to make their time worthwhile. The last report from Dalbar, which is actually very similar to the prior year's reports that they have done, found that investors averaged a 2.4% annual rate of return. That's right. They averaged 6.6% less than if they would have just bought an S&P 500 index type fund and left it alone. That is remarkable. Let me share an idea of what that means in real dollars.

Assume an investor had a stock portfolio worth $250,000 for a 20-year period of time. At a hypothetical 9% average growth rate that account would reach roughly $1,400,000. At just 2.4% it would grow to a mere $400,000 making a $1,000,000 loss of earnings in just 20 years. And that doesn't include all the time and effort on the part of the investor. How is this possible? How can investors do so poorly while the very markets they are investing in do so much better? The answer did not surprise me.

It is because investors are emotional creatures. The S&P 500 average rerturns over 30 years assumes you never touch your investment, but real humans have a very difficult time doing that. Real people feel real emotions, especially the dangerous ones of fear and greed. Dalbar has continually discovered that investors in general stocks tend to pull their money in and out of the markets or in and out of individual stocks based on the emotions of the season. Sadly, they tend to be very good at moving positions at the wrong times. They are wrong so regularly that the differences in returns are staggering.

There is another annual report on investor behavior and this one comes from Fidelity Investments. This report compares investors who buy strictly index funds on their own versus investors who use a professional financial advisor. The purpose of this report is to determine the value of financial advice to see if it is worth paying for. In their study, Fidelity researchers determined that using a financial advisor will generally result in a 3% per year higher rate of return. This again is a remarkable number because it takes into account the average advisor fees.

What's important in this particular report is why it is that advisors can earn you more money than you earn on your own. Once again, over a period of 20 years starting with a portfolio of $250,000, an additional 3% of return will amount to an additional $200,000 in portfolio value. That is no small amount. So what are financial advisors doing differently? Are they really that much better at picking stocks than an average investor? I would say not necessarily. According to the researchers, there appears to be two main differences between a professionally and a personally managed account. #1-advisors were better at creating and maintaining a well-balanced portfolio, which helped their clients avoid the worst of the volatility. #2 – Advisors managed their client's expectations and emotions, keeping them from making the mistake of pulling out their money in times of fear, or getting greedy and taking undo risk when things were good. The advisors weren't just managing the investments, they were managing the client. Based on the results of Dalbar as described above, the biggest risk to an investor is usually him or herself. #3 – Advisors used strategies such as tax harvesting and dollar cost averaging, as well as selective selling when clients needed to take draws, so that the returns were not harmed by unwise money movements. This practice is also known as "sequencing" and considers the value of the order in which assets are bought or redeemed. How an individual sequences additions and withdrawals from an account can have a measurable effect on total return.

Our home used to back up to a farmer's field and we learned that the farmer would adjust the exact day of planting based on the unique weather that year. At the end of the season he would carefully select the best day to harvest based on temperature and moisture in the air. These small adjustments resulted in significant improvements in the farmer's crop.

It has been my repeated experience as I have watched our clients and our CFP® professionals, that our team continually helps people to not make poor decisions. We certainly spend significant effort attempting to find great investments, but all this effort is for naught if the client takes over and insists on making investment decisions at the wrong time. Economic disasters, and booms for that matter, tend to be short-lived but far too many investors get burned by rushing into decisions because of them.

The truth is, no one knows if a stock or even if a specific market will go up or down in the coming year. The value of investing is based on using long term averages and experience to work in your favor. If we can keep our clients invested in well-allocated positions, and manage inflows and outflows in market efficient and tax efficient manners, we can earn our worth. That is where Fidelity researchers estimated that extra 3% comes from.

All of this brings me to a valuable lesson a client taught me when I was young in this business. A lesson which changed the way I view my relationship with my clients and my value to them, and resulted in Wyson Financial becoming the successful financial advisory firm that it is today.

This story begins when I was teaching financial seminars on a weekly basis at various locations in the three states where I was licensed at the time. It was my belief then, and remains so today, that I am first and foremost, an educator. Perhaps the worst thing that can happen in my office is that a person comes to us for advice, we carefully provide that advice and execute a plan, then a year or so later the client decides to take their money elsewhere. When this happens, the client is not served as any good financial plan takes many years to properly develop. Financial planning is not just a marathon, it is a lifetime process that requires many years for all the pieces to come together. As Dalbar and Fidelity have shown year after year, it requires consistency in sticking with a plan in the face of both fearful and greedy markets.

If a client leaves after a short while for whatever reason, they have not given the plan time to develop, or the markets time to go through the several cycles necessary to reach the average returns that are planned for. I cannot stress enough that investing takes time and patience and the cost for not being willing to dedicate both can be, as described above, very significant.

So, at an educational seminar series held at a local private community, there was a gentleman who quietly attended for almost a year. He was always cordial but rarely made comments or asked questions. Every week he sat near the back with his notebook and pen, frequently writing as I led discussions on various investment topics. I would greet him when he arrived and wish him well as he left, always offering to provide more personal financial services should he ever want them, but he would politely decline. Over the year I had gathered he was a wealthy and experienced investor who was largely looking to expand his knowledge but seemed to prefer continuing to do the investing on his own. He was clearly a do-it-yourselfer, a type of investor that I have great respect for, knowing how much effort it requires.

As a fulltime financial advisor, I have access to substantial resources that we are able to acquire using economies of scale. I also have relationships with key industry professionals that I can tap when specialized information or help is needed. But maybe most importantly, an individual investor must rely on their own life's experience in making investment decisions. A financial advisor with a large book of business has the benefit of learning from the successes and failures of the thousands of people with whom they work and interact over many years. We have seen what works and what doesn't in literally thousands of cases. We have seen how markets rise and fall and how those two affect portfolios over time. We have learned from the mistakes of those who acted rashly, what not to do. No matter how much an individual tries, they will always lack the volume of sheer experience a longtime financial advisor will have through the hundreds and thousands of accounts that they manage.

After a seminar I taught that related to fraud, this gentleman approached me and thanked me for some comments I had made that he felt he wanted to pass on to some members of his family. Over the course of our visit, I asked him why he continued to come to my meetings. What was he hoping to learn? His response was enlightening, and it stuck with me. He said, "I know a great deal about investing, but I don't know what I don't know. I come here to learn what questions I should be asking." He went on to explain that he was a very educated investor and he did significant research before making any purchases or changes. But the one thing that always weighed on his mind was, "What am I missing? What am I not even thinking about?" He felt confident he could find the answer to any question, but what if he didn't know the question to ask? I asked him, "And have I answered the unasked question?" His reply surprised me. "Yes, you have," he said, "Many times." And with that he handed me a printout of his entire portfolio and asked me to take over its management.

That experience led me to frequently ponder his comment. What is it that I am not asking? We have listed so far in this book 8 questions we get asked all the time, but what about those important questions that our clients or potential clients never think to ask? Those may be the most important to ask, and also the most dangerous to overlook.

The sheer volume of work that we do; the large amounts of money that we manage; the thousands of investors we have worked with over the years; the countless hours meeting privately with heads of industry; the long conversations helping clients not to get greedy when things are good; the emotional visits with clients encouraging them to stay the course when world events make them fearful; and a hundred other matters and issues that we deal with on a regular basis, put us in a position to ascertain each client's individual 9th question. When we do a review of a person's goals, needs and resources, we come to know what critical question that client has not yet asked, and how to answer it. The 8 questions in this book are common to our work and to many of our clients, but the 9th question is unique to each investor and often holds the key to that person's investing success. Finding the answer is not difficult. Discovering the question is the challenge. But doing so is what makes being a Certified Financial Planner™ so worthwhile, because that extra 3% can change lives.

CONCLUSION

I am a pilot. I can think of no better analogy to financial planning than flying an airplane. I love flying and what I love most about it is the freedom it gives me. As a pilot I can just about go anywhere I want, pretty much anytime I want to go there. In order to do so I must have a high level of respect for the physical laws that make flight possible. I have to assure that I am personally fit for the mission. I have to maintain and inspect my aircraft to confirm that it is also prepared for the flight. I must carefully review the weather and confirm that not only is it safe to fly, but that I and my airplane are prepared and suited for the challenges the weather may present each day.

Finally, I need to diligently train, keeping my skills sharp, so that in the event something goes wrong – and things do go wrong – I am prepared to adjust my plans so that a positive outcome of the flight will still occur. Only by doing these things can I truly enjoy the freedom and the benefits of flight. I had a very wise flight instructor say to me, "In flying there are no amateurs - At least none who will live very long. We all must be professional pilots. And if we are not willing to be a professional, we must hire a pilot who is." I have taken that advice to heart and always treated flying in a highly professional manner. And I will say that for many years I and my family have truly enjoyed the freedom of flight and the many glorious journeys we have taken together.

And so it is with financial planning and investment management. There are laws that apply and rules that must be followed. We must learn the laws and train for our mission. We must apply proper practices and stick to them. We must, in investing, be and act like professionals. Or, we should hire a professional to do it for us.

In this book you have heard some of our most commonly asked questions. You have read our partial answers to those questions. Hopefully you have gained some insight into some of the questions you have had. Maybe even more importantly you have been led to ask a few questions of your own. Maybe you have even discovered your own 9th question. That missing piece of your financial puzzle that may help it all come together.

Hopefully along the way I have succeeded in reminding you to stay focused on the very purpose for why we invest. It is about lifestyle. It is about happiness. It is about the ability to make the lives of others better. It is about the confidence that comes from having our financial house in order. It is about the freedom of flight and the glorious destination a well thought out and professionally executed financial plan can give you. Poor financial management is one of the leading causes of stress in life. Having your financial life built on a solid foundation can give you the freedom and the wherewithal to do many of those things in life that you enjoy, with those people who you most enjoy being with. It starts with asking, and answering, the right questions.

Do you have a question not answered in this book? Please write to us and we will respond and maybe even include your question in the next issue.

Info@WysonFinancial.com